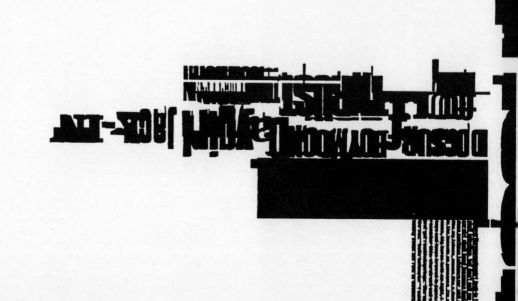

written and designed by karl hyde
and john warwicker of
underworld/tomato ▬▬▬▬▬

first published by booth-clibborn
editions, october 1994 ▬▬▬▬▬▬
re-printed october 1997 ▬▬▬▬▬
re-printed october 1999 ▬▬▬▬

distributed worldwide by Internos
books, 12 percy street, london w1p
9fb, uk ▬▬▬▬▬▬▬

usa rights reserved ▬▬▬▬▬

distributed in france by InterArt
Paris, 1 rue de l'est, 75020 paris,
france ▬▬▬▬▬▬▬▬

printed in the uk ▬▬▬▬▬

ISBN 1873968 582 ▬▬▬▬▬

...clusterm and trigger. 30,000 feet above the earth, the last day, no words necessary. just shocked to realise i'd given up believing this could happen. pen and trilling sunset pump tank and elvis. here comes moscow, mouth burning for sweet jeanita and shanty town days and the pump. boy relishing the trash elvis sings skyline cowboy talking black, your eyes and the hungry bull game from raw, are tater in hubble pure redemption rockstar. i would have derailed sky. 2panecame the other for her eyes. stars blazing solitary and nothing less. speedfan and breathing live spoke-eyes sisterroom her face. i could turn 400 into a thousand if i wasn't geared in furniture. clears gun, leaks across swimming with insects. steel pics and everything softness the money, sea of blonde and rockdrill. your name next mountain, trust me. jack in. fzz super ssis dena the net flottering bands across the face of the black girl blonde in the blood click old virus, liquid frown, and you i need guild. another - held from and real stuff, same eyes tomorrow beyond binary the ordinary woman. rise shark kittini and the steel of wet wince - fan, threshfor as loud as you in a digital fortune. its lightme. redsnakennked and clouded - efficiency woman. don't want you, i need your future kitten. don't talentt head in the sky. same to disk. the keys are getting shorter, deport - fretted fretid - a question or more. fuck your shit, just a closed-loop. dirty wonderful thrust space and silence of memory gloss. fire a star. tacky tacky. a parliment of crows trying naked in er under your shit. number 13 rifle. sanitissed and crusted. and the men is white. tacky and the mony in my head. she said. number 13 rifle. sometimes i cry. you're never lost in the sky. sanitissed and crusted. and the

Daygirl jack

TOUCHTOWN

baby baby b

jack morei

i'm invisible

1101011101101101011101101101
01011101101101011101011101101
0101010101011101101

0101101011011001011101
01011001011101
1110101

0101

#2

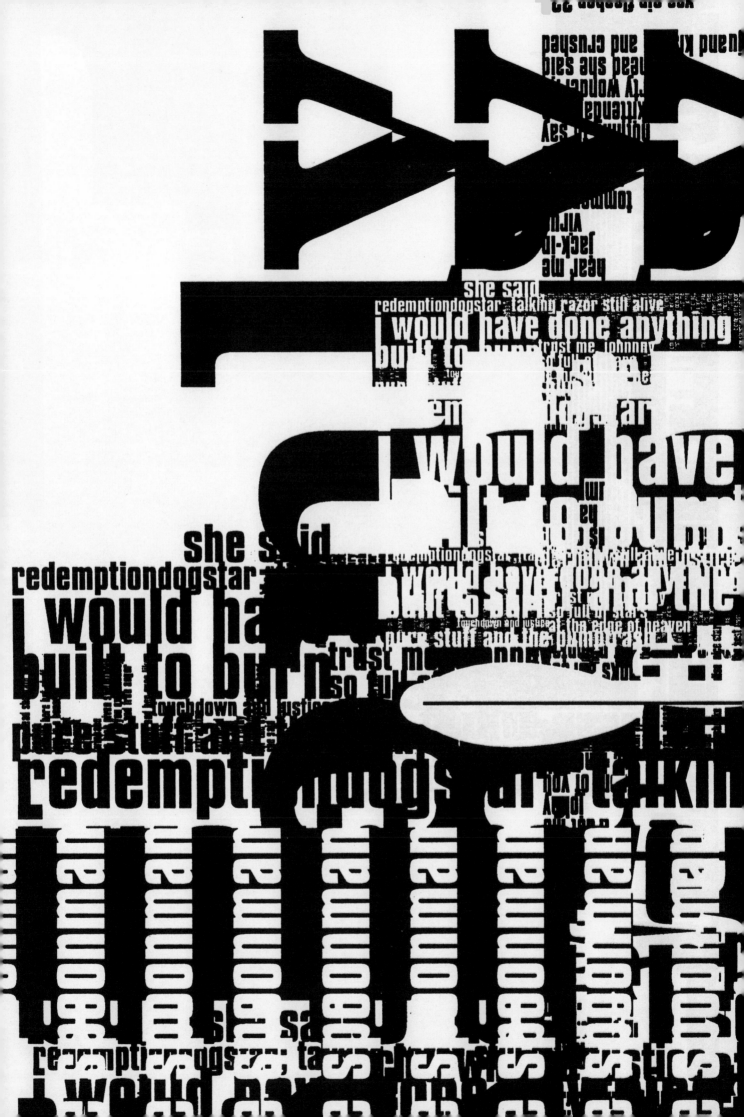

girl and hotel that

how fast

i'm invisi
i'm invisi
i'm invisi
m invisi
m invisi
m invisi
m invisi
m invisi

of longer hair

(and)

told him.

and

and

and

and

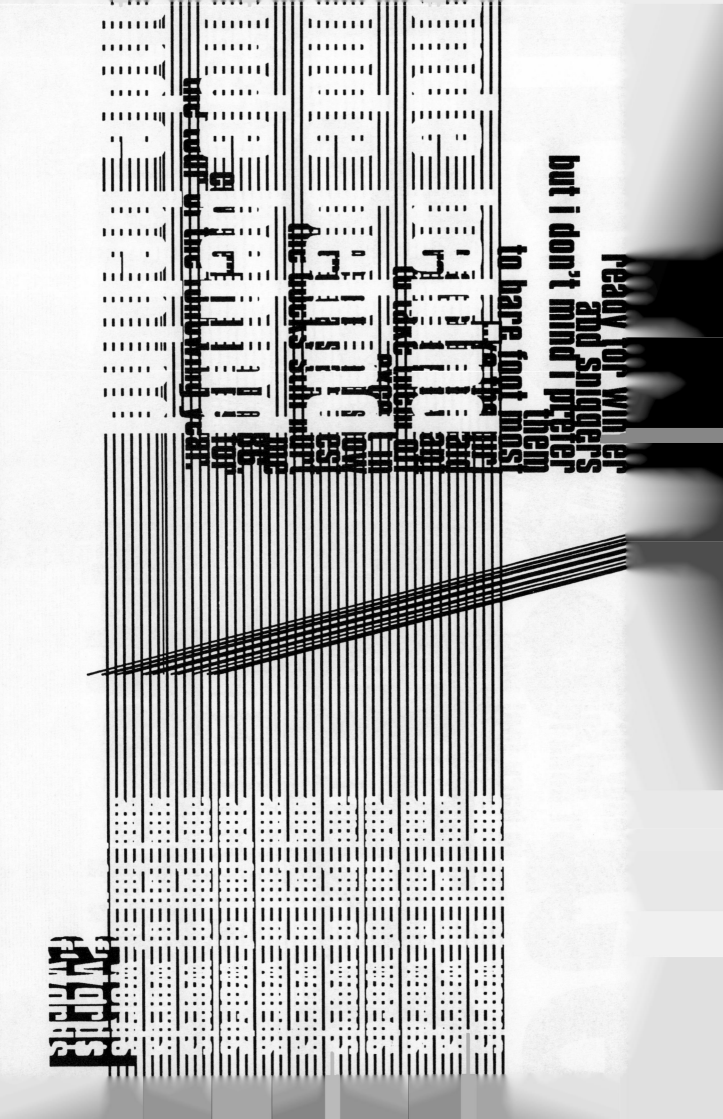

inking

x and

i feel;
the crackdown

CKED 4

that numbness here in front

i don't know whether you will understand
but
i want you 2pressure me numb
softsoftbabepre
snakecharm and messedupjohnny go
hunting dark
so give us what we want just do itdog a

bone
crawl

pop !

my first lil elvis

collapse

in stereo silence und

just give me everything

...te and snake through si

yes sir 09 93 re +	binaryboys
under the 40	bikini and the bitemeat
highdensity honey	fluxhead folios
massive bitten	silenthead in the dogwings
built to burn	lying
fist of london seduced in	shaken
codes	in the sallad
full thrust	number15 and the thing
nowords necessary	talk
purestuff and the pumptrash	this plane is ready
rawbathing kingrazor	realburn and cowboy
still loving	centuryskin feels honey
solid tan	forever
feel my face	city whip somestumbled into
if i wasn;t steel pins	first loneliness old cowboy
if i wasn	trust me
fax me	johny
	infront of you
	don't call me kingdrill
	the cargirl breathing snake
	eyes
	sister chews gum
	looks across
	ypur move next moontan
	trust me
	blonde is the blond

sible

cowa

ten he

100110101010101
10101010101010

xby baby im

an old cowboy
he
was
theredempti
i would have
talking razo
for you

under tha w
blonde is the
bamboo
elvis-the vir
liquid trees
i need solid
glamourglos
a lacky
a parliment
lying in the
hello helico
i said
there's a ga
rain

...addess working in a
returant she aked me to
be on a quiz show she
took me to the make-up
room and started kissing
me all over this is
delicious channel 69 the
ultimate extension of
hard rock and smart drugs
wind speed rising summers
lets this year 2 snakes
in a bed children of god
keep your eye on the ball
this is the big meat show
adult filmstar welcome
one and all black earth
rising stone to the bone
lets take a ride lets
shake and dive black
earth rising stone to the
bone lets take a ride
lets burn some rubber
touchdown crawl across
the floor touch down give
me some more touch down
crawl along the floor
lets burn some rubber and
ride children of god keep
your eye on the ball up
on the cross its the big
meat show theres room for
more this is the big meat
show adult filmstar
channel 69 fast food to
go the big meat show
adult filmstar channel 69
fast food to go natural
obsession delicious smile
natural obsession
channel69

soldier like footsteps on ash deep green counting the numbers of deliverance running for the overground

timing circles peaceful diguised as a stolen radio stone against the window 00:30 phone rings pick it up raw

white van the sound of a locked briefcase boy makes the sound of exploding water of steam of perculated

coffee following the receeding reflection of hair in glass makes the sound of a cat he goes "aaaah!" makes

the sound of a volcano "no" he goes sound like a fizz like smoke sounds like a hi hat into the tunnel beneath

your black jeans frayed at the balls the herd running meat with its head waiting for rain woman with a gold

dog smiling smelling of ditchleaves pulls a bag down a string of pearls just the ticket woman with a gold dog

reflected in glass face swolen with sandwhich boy explodes like boiled water makes the sound "peep!"

eating the herd the suits the woman black and white piston quaker hissing loose change exchanging hands

like it does numbers woman with a gold dog tin foil boy make the sound like a rattlesnakehorn the herd

turns undecided gathering at the wire brings the smell of fart from the arse of the golden dog lingering

pistons boy makes the sound of an espresso machine like a metal trolley on a grating says "mmm box" and

another fart from the arse of the golden dog beneath you tunnel boy makes the sound of rattlesnake of

horn fox breader hatcher tiny conceled railrust gathering circling boy makes boy makes the sound of an

electric razor says "gas mask" pigeon floodlit on a stick laughs in leather boy makes a fizz makes another

snare drum roll tape turned on a walkman waiting hissing sleepers in the weeds shirts and girls shiney

bags above thier heads laughing shiney shiney smelling of fresh wind briefcase rainbow spandex crossed

below the waste beneath an open book piston whistle horn orange bag denhim girl cut offs curled up the

glass sleeping ticket man cuts pieces out like a #2 swolensuits woman checks her hair gold buttons tidy

lines nice shirt man up her arm ballancing fresh coffee coming shiney shiney shoe pump woman makes

piston noises persued by recleding hair all hands on handles waiting circling sniffing mirror on a stick

chocolate infusion horn red hair flag falls from the back of the seat infront arse of the golden dog cheese

chilli ham egg bacon egg cheese tomato soft drinks egg bacon ham drink or anything tea coffee 75 what you

got needs 3 in 1 sir black or white sir sleepers laughing weeds plastic orange piston parking perfumed horn

fluttering baghead horns bells smelling of burnt chocolate piston iston

love

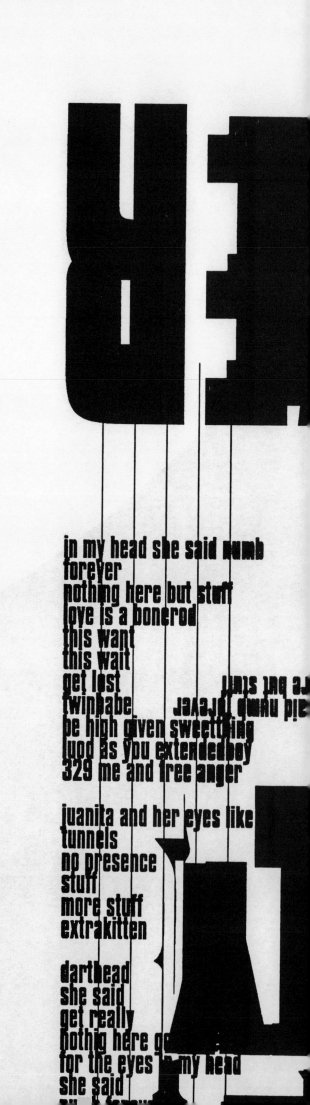

in my head she said numb
forever
nothing here but stuff
love is a bonerod
this want
this wait
get lost
twinbabe
be high given sweetthing
luod as you extendedboy
329 me and free anger

juanita and her eyes like
tunnels
no presence
stuff
more stuff
extrakitten

darthead
she said
get really
nothig here ge
for the eyes in my head
she said

it

itthe taxman i earn
such little money
where are we
stratfoed i can't
believe it takes
this long to get to
stratford there's
no more fighting i
try to get away
from dark
double-acts floral
skirts unusual pink
nighties oh god
you've never seen i
dunno seeyou see
you sunday 11 at
finchley bye

she said,
redemptiondogstar; talking ra
i would have do
built to burn trust me, jo
so full of sta
touchdown and justice at the end da
pure stuff and the burning

i'm the

i'm the

i'm the
she sa
redemptiondogstar; ta
i would hav
built to bur
touchdown and ju
pure stuff and t
d o

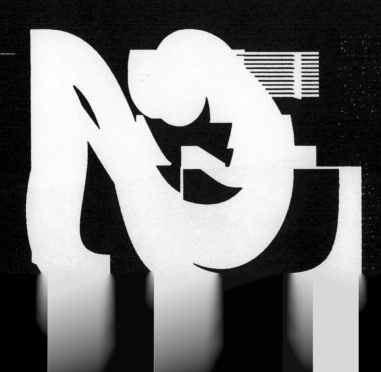

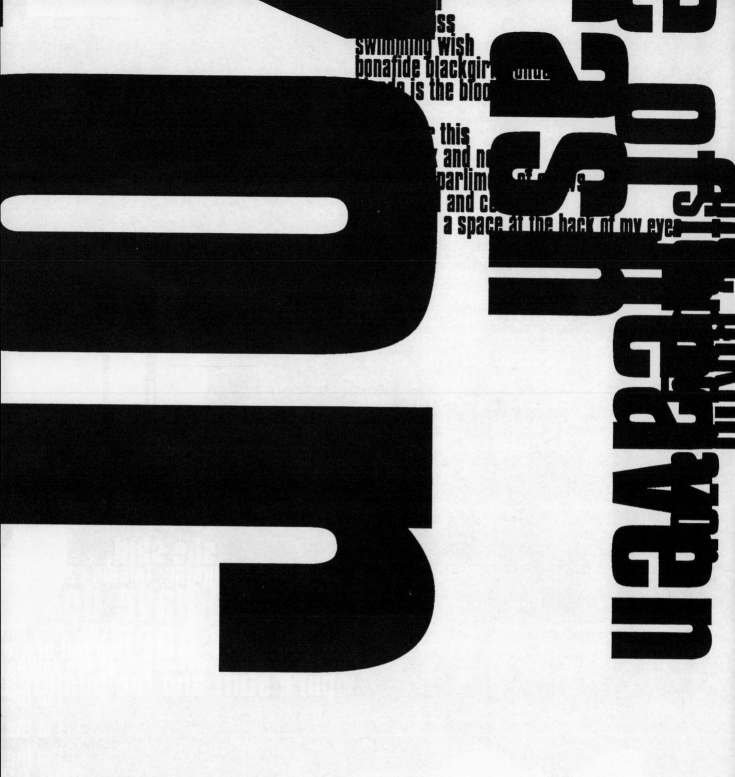

swimming wish
bonafide blackgirl ... blue
... is the bloo...

... this
... and n...
parlim... ...
and c...
a space at the back of my eyes

skyscraper

fl and hotelbabes

ow fast are

re

i'minvisible
i'minvisible
i'minvisible
i'minvisible
i'minvisible
i'minvisible
i'minvisible
i'minvisible

the earth. the best day, no words necessary. just shocked to realise i'd given up believing this could happen. pure
. here comes moscow.groombigburning for sweet juanita and shanty town dogs and the pump boy polishing. the
'ng black.pony rise and the honey hunt come down raw. arc bathe in bubble pure redemptiondogstar. i would have
her eyes, stars moving solitary.and nothing less. speedjam and breathing like snake-eyes sisterraygun her face
asn't covered in furinlove, chews gum, looks across swimming with insects, steel pins and everything softtones
ill, your move next moontan, trust me. jack-in. fax super asia down the net.fluttering hands across the face of the
d virus. liquid trees and you i need solid.another hotel room and real stuff. same eyes tomorrow beyond.binary
the steel of wet minds. dan. birdstar as loud as god in a digital future. it's bigtime.redsnakenohead and cloudhat
rt want you, i need youextrakitten. dark talent head in the sky. save to disk. the days are getting shorter.dogsoul
rty wonderful.thrash space and silence glamourgless. like a star. lacky lacky. a parliment of crows lying naked in
d like. sometimes i cry. you're never lost in the sky. sunkissed and crushed. and the room is white. beauty and the

nice shark
tommorrow
virus
jack-in
hear me
no expert
insects
sisterraygun into a thousar
do anything
church of hunt come down
shantydog
pumptank
happen
the best day no words coul
daygirl jack-in

talk
eyes
stars

DOGSOUL BOYMOON

daygirl

PRIEST TOUGHTOWN

30,000 feet above

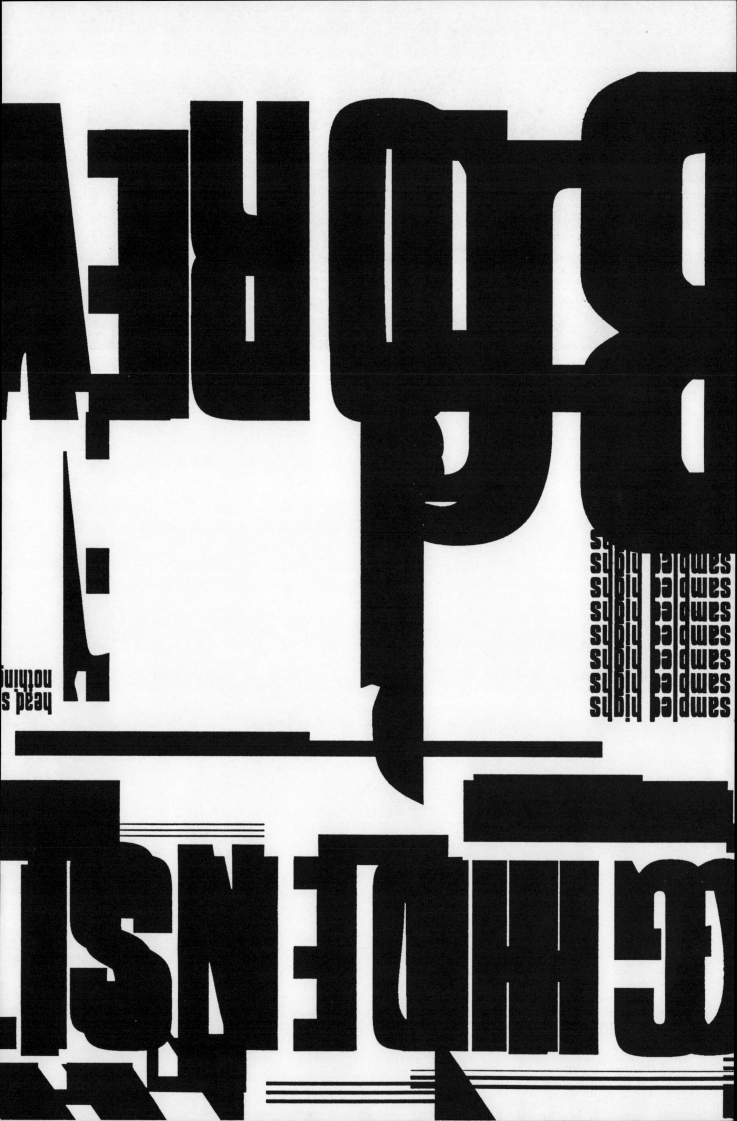

i need solid

you are the blade
on which
i cut my self

al lolita derail me every time. talking

this is my beautiful dream

kiss me

cowgirl forever and ever l

talking dog speed in the sn

and snow sync to so

teenage sex and stoned rhythm tradi

jack-in and call

i feel; like fly

come kiss hurting on the crackdown

juST SHOCKED 4 HEAL

that numbers here in front ju

that numbness here in front ju

i don't know whether you will understand

but

i want you 2pressure me numb

softsoftbabepress

snakecharm and messedupjohnny go

hunting dark

so give us what we want just do itdog and

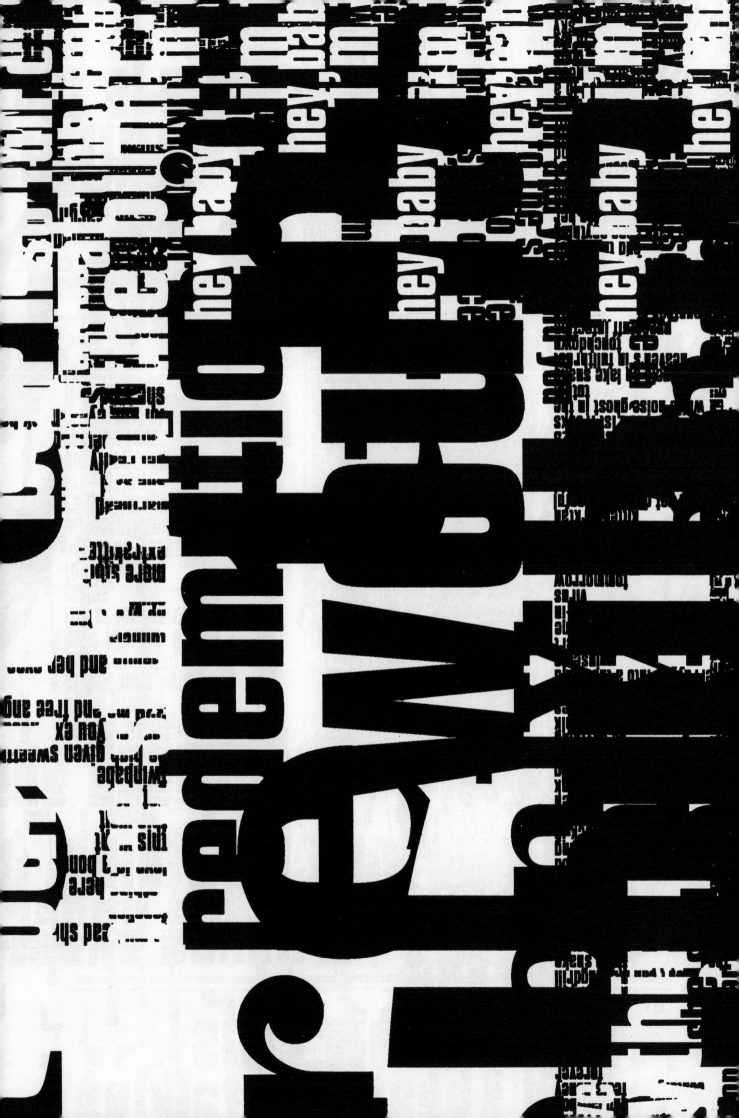

and a...u...
exploding it's written
built in lipstick
silent tears speak

extracting curves

one the city run

fuckit we're all going to euroc
spiders crawling like spiders up the w
the her red jacket saturdatnightsund
s aly on the phone i'm more open we
stooped or bloody skin or swim like lip
the smell of your coat away we can't st
woman in a big hair coat blue anorack
london accessory 93 blondebomb gol pl
contents of a dubious briefase i smell c
nicotine00:25:21 12 92 late new me eit
piss glass and plastic thinking of you
needle perfect o... sealed with a kiss d
o take me back to elvis its the big tim
fuckingpisshead 1993answer the door l
sweetforce wetlands atlantic cross i sr
discreet rubberfriend quick random ac
deepdreampeace harmony blonde leath
like a cool hand chanhassen country in
except the bits you can't see normally
yellow spidertits like tapioca

redemptiondogs
would
built to
touchdov
pure $uff a
you're

done anything
ust me, johnny
full of stars
f the edge of heaven

or still alive
ne anything
e, johnny
of stars
dge of heaven

realise
i'd give
don't call
sneer burning
for the cargirl
boytalking
redemptiondogbrand
speed
jam
and breed

dancer and smiler
urinlove
chews softones in the
rockdrill
your fluttering hands
blackgirl
another hotel
in japan
he minds
danbirdhatremember
more i don't
the days are under your
glosshelicopter
i said
you're never beauty
and collapse
than i thought they land
the snow and rain
09 93
re-heart starkland

stuff and more stuff
bone blue
jug
have already
codes
sampled boy
has he got gone
hope
just shocked to realise
i'd
here comes
bigburning
foreverelvis sings
skyline hot cowboy live
under moves the dancer
smiles
and
everything in softones

a
couple of people
said to me before
that i'm quite
threatening and i'm
just normal he
needs to be
directed that's why
i suggested getting
him back to my
place who does the
childrens pictures
you remember that
bloke who took his
jacket off this
week and you said
oh yeah i wishthat
bloke wouldtake his
jacket off he knows
how to tell a story
about sex it would
be i think he would
enjoy it oh yeah we
very rarely have
vocal argumentative
rows and we have
this argument every
day when i've been
painting he's like
a dead soul inside
living flesh and i
feel he meybe feels
threatened by i
       know maybe i
       to work out
       him you know i
       know but he's
       y good bloke
       got realy tiny
       ry hands poor
       sounds like
       ing out of a
       chook places

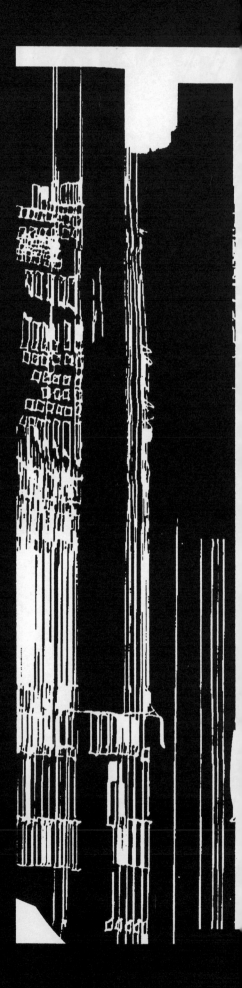

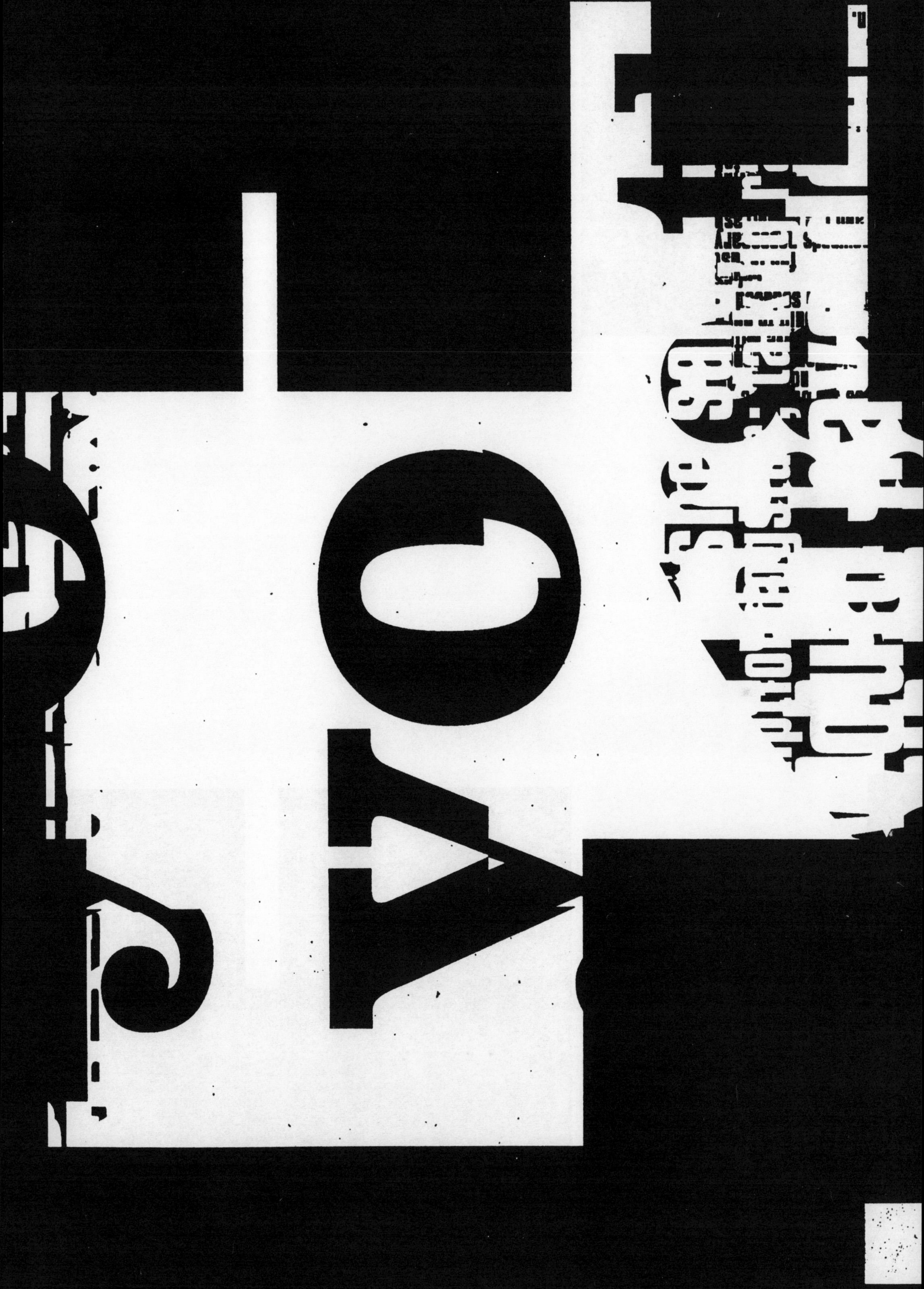

no3 no5 no7 no15
the room next door cries like a baby unsalted butter max
lights on

It's been so hard since I done anything right I can't remember working hard to make you happy you were a beautiful creature a snake with lights

my busy to play.

and fart

and and and and

talk to me talk to my machi

naked
blonde

30,000feet above the earth its a beaut_ful thing and your a beautiful thing
30,000feet above the earth and everybodys a beautiful thing and i see elvis and
i hear god on the phone elvis talking to god on the phone i see porndogs
sniffing the wind sniffing the wind for something new porn dogs sniffing the
wind for something violent they can do porn dogs sniffing the wind sniffing the
wind for something new porn dogs sniffing the wind for something violent for
me and you the city is a whore tonight will you be my big plaything my total
big disorientater will you be my big plaything my ninja power my number
cruncher and i see elvis and i hear god on the phone pornfest pork fat jesus
christ nightlight elvis fresh meat and a little whipped cream 30,000 feet above
the earth its a beautiful thing and your a beautiful thing 30,000 feet above the
earth its a beautiful thing and your a and everybodys a beautiful thing

ouldn't put
our face she
aid a dollar
ubber rat utah
lates brilliant
reen substance
nknown with a
ace like a
eeled onion
heep in drag
orschachantom

e the screamers
orschachantom

he rolling

boy baby
baby
boy

in my head she said numb
sweet stuff

but stuff
numb forever
sweetthing
extendedboy
free anger

juanita and her eyes like

extrakitten

darthead
she said
get really
nothig here go
for the eyes in my head
she said
numb foreve...

Daygirl jack-in

ST

MU?

realise
i'd give
don't call
sneer burning
for the cargirl
boytalking
redemptiondogbrand
speed
jam
and breed

dancer and smiler
grinlove
chews softones in the
rockdrill
your fluttering hands
blackgirl
another hotel
in japan
he minds
danbirdhatremember
more i don't
the days are under your skin
glosshelicopter
i said
you're never beauty
and collapse
than i thought they land
the snow and rain
09 93
re-heart starkland

stuff and more stuff
bone blue
jug
have already
codes
sampled boy
has he got gone
hope
just shocked to realise
i'd
here comes
bigburning
foreverelvis sings
skyline hot cowboy live
under moves the dancer
smiles
and
everything in softened

another
i don't
i need
just a c
i said
there's
and a b
then
snow a
welcom
sharkh
gbabes
i'm exp
thighs
she wa
s
pumpta
here co
sweet t
still ali
nder t
with ins
steel pi
and
everyth
softone

i need s
another
question
or
more
i don't w
i need y

the sun
hello
helicopt
i said
here's
head sub
this is a
livehaer

couldn't put
your face she
said a dollar
rubber rat utah
plates brilliant
green substance
unknown with a
face like a
peeled onion
sheep in drag
horsebachantom
little to make
your home clean
make it
sanni-flush she
said now I'm a
new skinfree
arlapy with this
urge to phone
into the
nonsmoking zone
of stainless
steel tokyo me
and big white
dog got to
hijack pecan
tarts for
abillion bambi
out of mercer
street where the
crackheads
catwalk for
charity where
teenage sex
rides a stoned
rythm trading
it's chillizkins
to the sorcerers
come to hunt
their meat to
the gold diggers
in kissboots and
the recycled
blondes in their
stack heeled
snatches the
monster trucks
the rolling
rocks the poodle
boys with their
little bone
diggers and
darkstuff comes
oozing out the
applecore
tonight like a
beggars dog
tasting the
wind

don't put your
hand where you
wouldn't put
your face she
said a dollar
rubber rat utah
plates brilliant
green substance
unknown with a
face like a
peeled onion
sheep in drag
horsebackuntom
attle to make
your home clean
make it
sanni-flush she
said now i'm a
new skinfree
crispy with this
urge to phone
into the
nosmoking zone
of stainless
steel tokyo me
and big white
dog get to
hijack pecan
tarts for
babillon bambi
out of mercer
street where the
crackheads
catwalk for
charity where
teenage sex
rides a stoned
rythm trading
it's chillichims
to the screemers
come to hunt
their meat to
the gold diggers
in kissboots and
the recycled
blondes in their
stack heeled
snatches the
monster trucks
the rolling
rocks the poodle
boys with their
little bone
diggers and
darkstuff comes
nosing out the
applecore
tonight like a
beggars dog
tasting the
wind

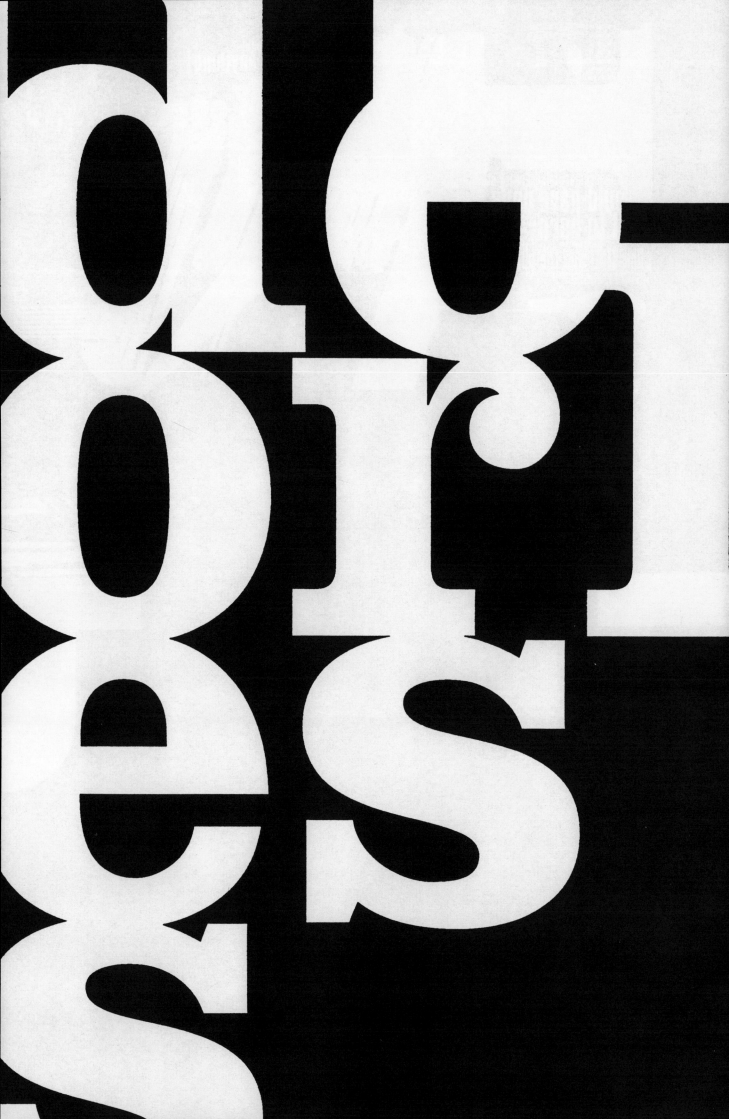

talking ra

have do

burn

trust me, johnnny

so full of stars

and justice at the edge of heaven

nd the bumblash

i'm the spoonman

i'm the spoonman

i'm the spoonman

she said

i'm the spoonman

demptiondogstar; talking razor still alive

would have done anything

built to burn

trust me, johnnny

so full of stars

touchdown and justice at the edge of heaven

ure stuff and the bumblash

tiondogstar; talk

uld have

burn

done anything

full of stars

the edge of heaven

umblash

razor still alive

just me, johnnny

ust of tears don't turn the

a
couple of people
said to me before
that i'm quite
threatening and i'm
just normal he
needs to be
directed that's why
i suggested getting
him back to my
place who does the
childrens pictures
you remember that
bloke who took his
jacket off this
week and you said
oh yeah i wishthat
bloke wouldtake his
jacket off he knows
how to tell a story
about sex it would
be i think he would
enjoy it oh yeah we
very rarely have
vocal argumentative
rows and we have
this argument every
day when i've been
painting he's like
a dead soul inside
living flesh and i
feel he meybe feels
threatened by i
don't know maybe i

i phoned just to listen to the sound of your voice dont say anything i have to go dont speak dont ask i cant seperated listening to the night train speak to me soft bend the rails i'm curled covered in wires

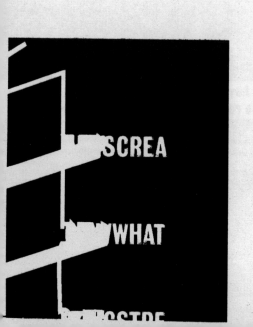

boy makes sound like a pig boy
makes sound like a bomb like a
like a snake like a machine sh
deep green counti IN HER of
deliverance

HAIR EYES LIKE
FANGS THROUGH
YOUR FACE SHE
SAYS   POWER
BEFORE PASSION
IN AND

ANGEL FROZEN   T FALLOU
MY STUPID MO   R FACE YOUR EYES
BETWEEN THE BARS RECEED

FANGS IN HER
HAIR EYES LIKE
FANGS THROUGH
YOUR FACE SHE
SAYS   POWER
BEFORE PASSION
IN AND

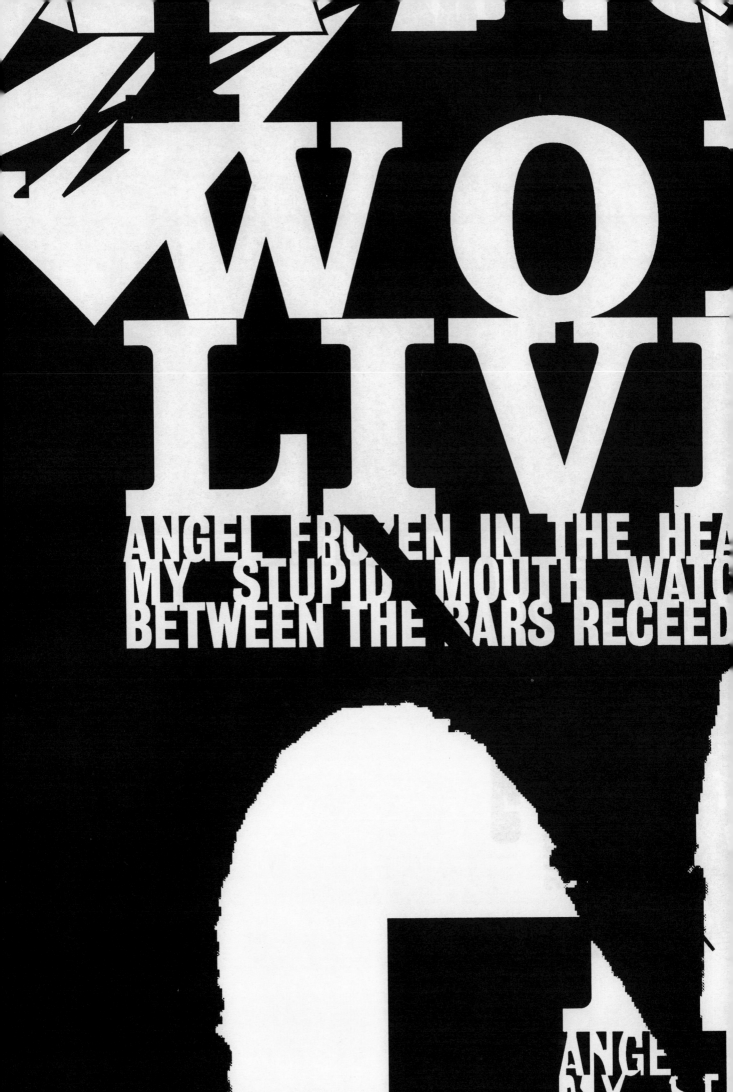

out,
and razor

SHE GOT RAYBANS IN HER HAIR EYES LIKE FANGS THROUGH YOUR FACE SHE SAYS POWER BEFORE PASSION IN AND

boy m
makes
like a
deep g
deliver

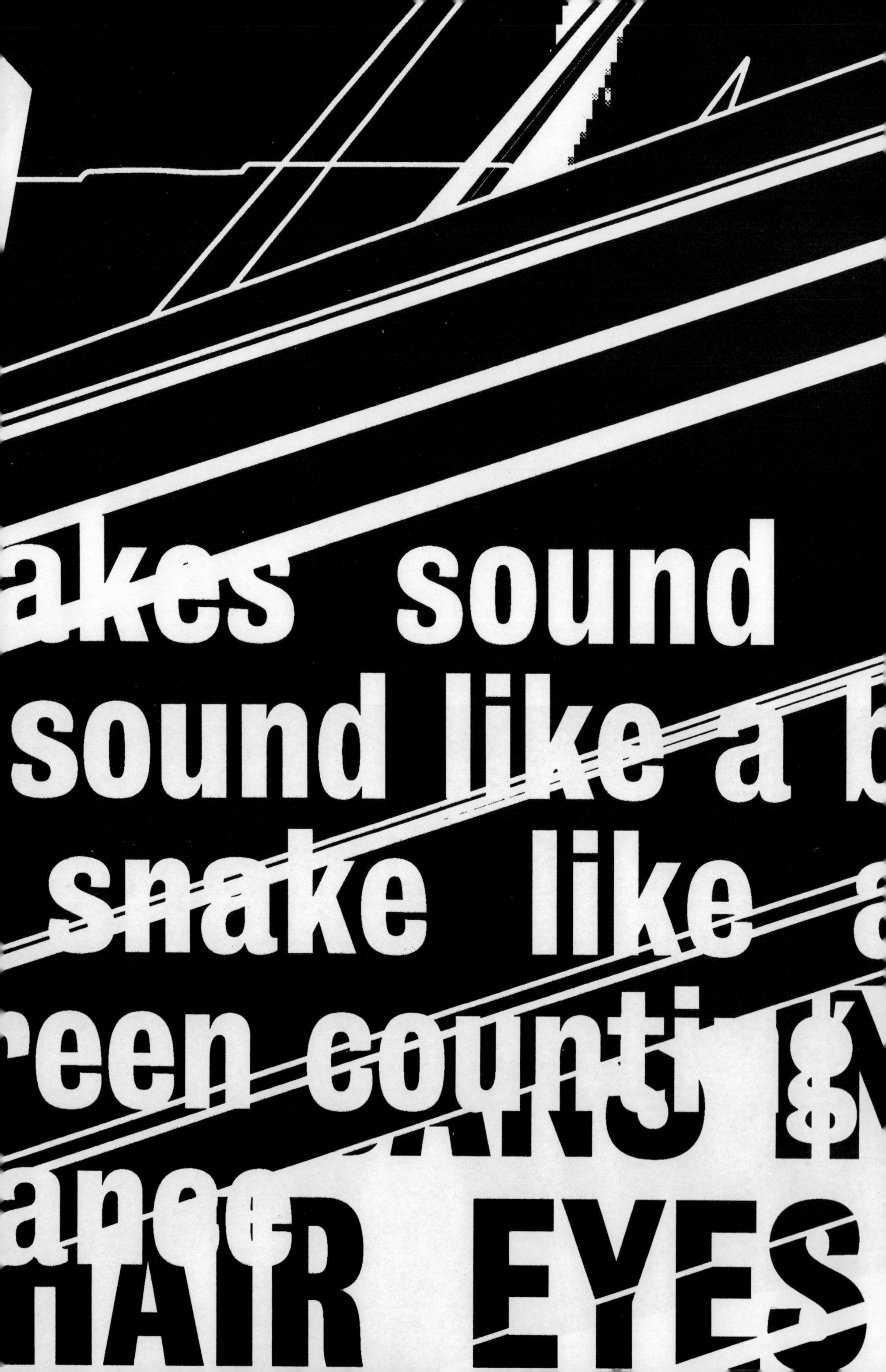

akes sound

sound like a b

snake like a

reen counti $

ano

AIR EYES

ANGEL FROZEN
MY STUPID M
BETWEEN THE

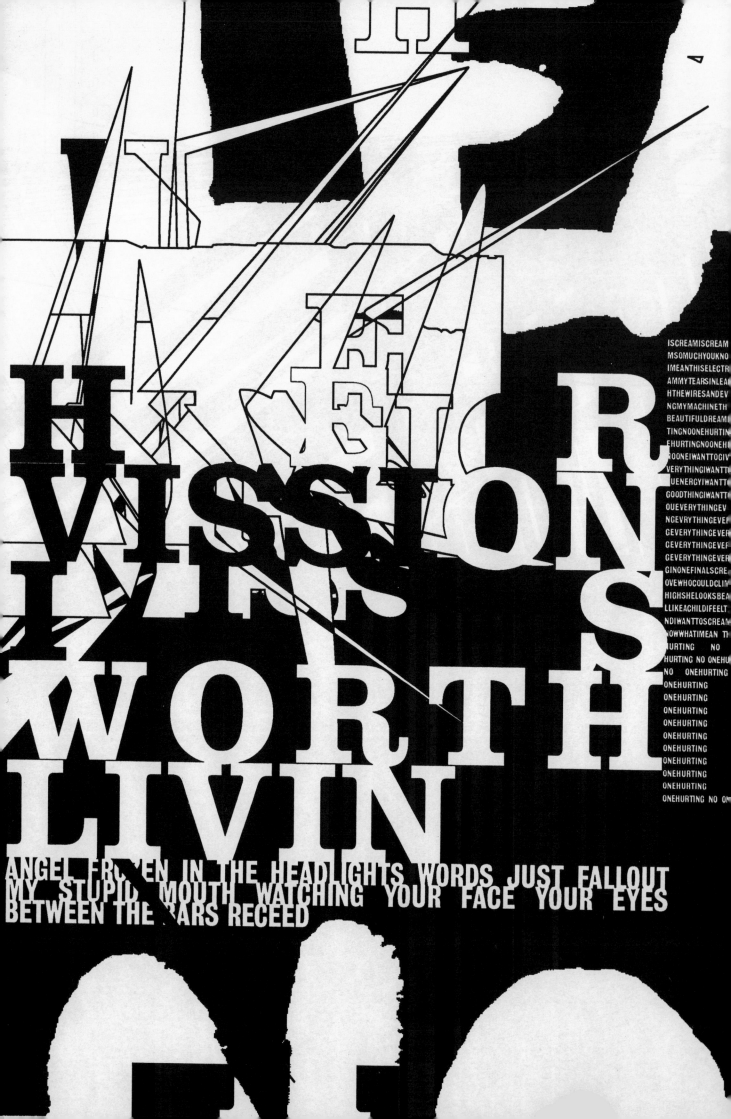

FANGS THR
YOUR FACE
SAYS
BEFORE PAS
IN AND

RS RECEED

was beautiful god

under the beauty expanse
starless and forever black

she was beautiful
she was beautiful
she was beautiful

and in w

extracting curves
and dark again
extended
everything

anger and the

MAKE A LOVE CONNECTION
TOUCHTONE REQUIRED BAD
BEAUTIFUL BUT SAVAGE X-T
SWEETER THAN SUGAR HOT
HARDER HOW MUCH FUN HAV
FOR RAW AS THE LAW ALLOW
BOXING OILWRESTLING FREE
WORLD OF SEXFAX FAXSUPE
BASEMENT OF WONDERLAND
PAGANFLOWER SAUNABAR B
SUPER 69 SEX CONNECT TH
TELEPHONE LAPDANCER PRO-
BIG AND BOUNCING STAND
ENCOUNTERS SINGLELADIES

...e a love connection the name says it all brand new never done before dr. heathr knows your needs touchtone required bad babes fall in lust sex connect hook up plug in turn on meet the boy next door beautiful but savage x-tasy uncensored talk hunk talk hardcorekinky always willing always accessible sweeter than sugar hot new series an afternoon delight alive and wild the best hardcore just got harder how much fun have you had lately women who take charge because you've been bad for that hot ride for raw as the law allows enter the dangerous world for that hot ride home strong gals lapdancing foxy boxing oilwrestling free buffet hot guys waiting now tops bottoms uniforms and more sizzle and burn world of sexfax faxsuperasia kandy's wonderwand mr. newmanbig big soft contact welcome welcome to the basement of wonderland erotic handlebars come welcome to my worm blonde blue jug babe wow 69 come paganflower saunabar barbi come in spanking yoko 4 devotional surrender wow in dick-o-matic macho super 69 sex connect the cutehunk china doll live fantasy the best things in life are still done by hand telephone lapdancer pro-jam lamb of god t-bird blow jobs on the verge elegant connections big gals live big and bouncing stand back you know what that spells hot 2 gal action live steaming hot selective encounters singleladies call free live hot meet attractive and professional singles tonight

S YOUR NE
OY NEXT D
S ACCASSA
ORE JUST
THAT HOT R
DANCING F
ZLE AND B
LCOME TO
WOW 69 CO
ATTIC MAC
DONE BY HA
BIG GALS L
OT SELECT
GLES TONIG

like a

a bomb like a b

a snake like a machine

green counting the numb

Dirty, mmm i love you

fluttering hands

and full of words
and full of words
and full of words
and full of words

Dirty, mmm i love y
Dirty, mmm i l
Dirty, mmm i
ty, mmm

Dirty, mmm i love fou

Dirty, mmm i lov

Dirty, mmm i

frozen

belief has gone again and left us all

belief has gone again and left us all

belief has gone again and left us all

has gone again

this girl derail this girl

derail

every time. talking

derail this every time. talking

nd razor

in.

ngel and the

eauty.

now

just to listen
to the sound
of your voice
just don't say
anything

trust me
we are full of stars

a mac

n hin talk

oe

al to

el me

nger in hotel

nore i don't

said

ever beauty

nd collapse

he snow

nd

30,000 feet above the earth
30,000 feet above the earth
30,000 feet above the earth
30,000 feet above the earth
30,000 feet above the earth
30,000 feet above the earth
30,000 feet above the earth
30,000 feet above the earth
30,000 feet above the earth
30,000 feet above the earth

like a snake like a machine ash
deep green counting the numbers of
deliverance

g for the overground timing circles peaceful diguised as a stolen
stone against the window 00:30 phone rings pick it up raw white
of exploding water running meat with its head waiting for rain

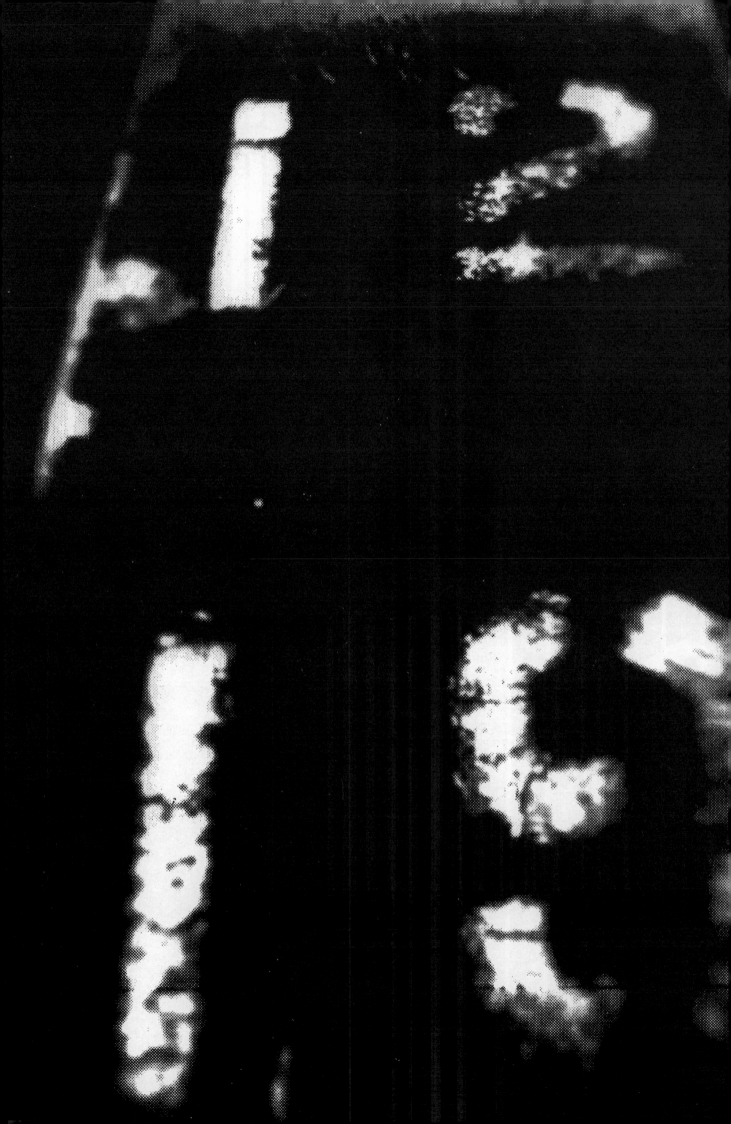

BUILDING WITH ITS GUTS OUT

SO WHATS THIS LIKE AN ANGEL FROZEN IN THE HEADLIGHTS WORDS JUST FALLOUT MY STUPID MOUTH WATCHING YOUR FACE YOUR EYES BETWEEN THE BARS RECEED

SHE GOT RAYBANS IN HER HAIR EYES LIKE FANGS THROUGH YOUR FACE SHE SAYS POWER BEFORE PASSION AND DRESSES LIKE A MASTERPLAN CLUTCHING A MAGAZINE LIKE A BULLETPROOFVEST SAYS "ESCAPE" ON THE BACK

ISCREAMISCREAMISCREAMSOMUCHYOUKNOWWHATIMEANTHISELECTRICSTREAMMYTEARSINLEAGUEWITHTHEWIRESANDEVERYTHINGMYMACHINETHISISMYBEAUTIFULDREAMI'MHURTINGNOONEHURTINGNOONEIWANTTOGIVEYOUEVERYTHINGIWANTTOGIVEAGOODTHINGIWANTTOGIVEYOUENERGYIWANTTOGIVEYOUEVERYTHINGEVERYTHINGNGEVERYTHINGEVERYTHINGEVERYTHINGINONEFINALSCREAMOFLOVEWHOCOULDCLIMBTHISHIGHSHELOOKSBEAUTIFULLIKEACHILDIFEELTEARSANDIWANTTOSCREAMYOUKNOWWHATIMEAN THIS IS HURTING NO ONE

HER VISION IS WORTH LIVING

e

come rain

c-to-sound

eleechesandju

ick

o me

elvis

ng burning

razor

er

10,000 feet above the earth

the feet above the earth

10,000 feet above the earth

10,000 feet above the earth

e liquid trees

folds a

ou

eboy in my
ve submassive
naller

eamed

Daygirl Jack

TOUGH TOWN

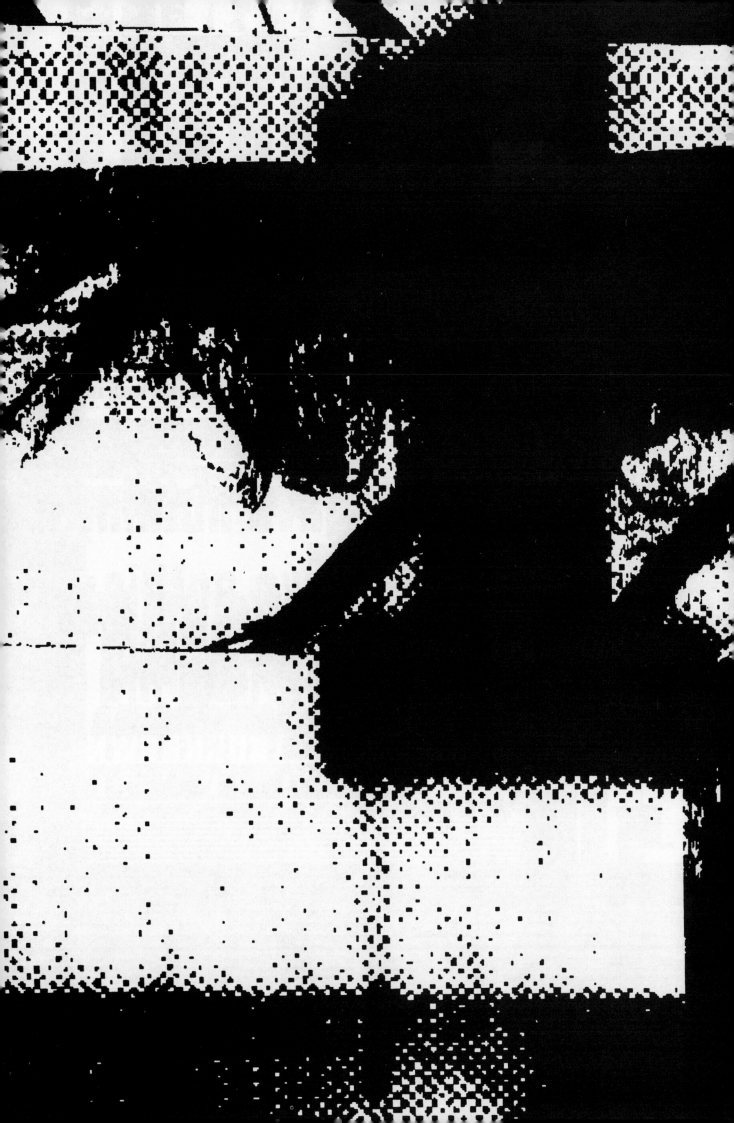

...he earth. the best day, no words necessary. just shocked to realise i'd given up believing this could happen. pure
...here comes moscow.groombigburning for sweet juanita and shanty town dogs and the pump boy polishing. the
...g black.pony rise and the honey hunt come down raw. arc bathe in bubble pure redemptiondogstar. i would ha...
...her eyes, stars moving solitary.and nothing less. speedjam and breathing like snake-eyes sisterraygun her fa...
...asn't covered in furiolove, chews gum, looks across.swimming with insects, steel pins and everything soften...
...ll. your move next moontan, trust me. jack-in. fax super asia down the net.fluttering hands across the face o...
...virus. liquid trees and you i need solid.another hotel room and real stuff. same eyes tomorrow beyond.bizar...
...the steel of wet minds. dan. birdstar as loud as god in a digital future. it's bigtime.redsnakenohead and cloud...
...'t want you, i need youextrakitten. dark talent head in the sky. save to disk. the days are getting shorter.dog...
...ty wonderful.thrash space and silence glamourgloss. like a star. lacky lacky. a parliment of crows lying nak...
...like. sometimes i cry. you're never lost in the sky. sunkissed and crushed. and the room is white. beauty and...

tommorrow
nice shark
virus
jack-in
hear me
no expert
insects
sisterraygun into a thousan...
stars
eyes
talk
do anything
church of hunt come down
shantydog
pumptank
happen
the best day no words could
daygirl jack-in

TRUST

TOUCHDOWN

naked a

you don't think about what you do you just do it what comes easy to you is hard

razor

kiss me